United States
Department of
Agriculture

Forest Service

Pacific Northwest
Research Station

General Technical
Report
PNW-GTR-842
April 2011

Giving Credit Where Credit Is Due: Increasing Landowner Compensation for Ecosystem Services

Gina L. LaRocco and Robert L. Deal

Authors

Gina L. LaRocco is a conservation program associate, Defenders of Wildlife, 1880 Willamette Falls Drive No. 200, West Linn, OR 97068; and **Robert L. Deal** is a research forester, U.S. Department of Agriculture, Forest Service, Pacific Northwest Research Station, Forestry Sciences Laboratory, 620 SW Main Street, Portland, OR 97205.

Cover: Prince of Wales Island, Alaska. Photo by Robert Deal.

Abstract

LaRocco, Gina L.; Deal, Robert L. 2011. Giving credit where credit is due: increasing landowner compensation for ecosystem services. Gen. Tech. Rep. PNW-GTR-842. Portland, OR: U.S. Department of Agriculture, Forest Service, Pacific Northwest Research Station. 32 p.

Conservation of biodiversity serves a number of human needs, including maintenance of ecosystem services that are critical to the sustainability of all life. Effective biodiversity conservation will require better landowner incentives for restoration and protection of ecosystems. Many services produced from healthy, functioning landscapes are not well recognized in current conservation incentive structures, including sequestering or storing carbon in trees and soil, providing fish and wildlife habitat, filtering water, and reducing damages from natural disasters. Most existing incentive programs pay landowners to protect and restore a specific service rather than the suite of services produced from well-functioning ecosystems. Various incentive programs need to be better integrated or new programs need to be developed that value a greater proportion of the ecological benefits that flow from ecosystems. One promising option is to allow landowners to bundle or stack payments for ecosystem services. This option, however, also presents issues that need to be addressed to ensure ecological goals and economic efficiency are achieved. Current efforts underway address some of these issues. Specifically, collaborative efforts among public and private entities in the Pacific Northwest and Chesapeake Bay region are developing accounting tools to measure ecosystem services and test policies for bundling services and stacking payments on the ground. The U.S. government has also made a commitment to ensure coordination and integration of ecosystem market development by creating a dedicated agency under the U.S. Department of Agriculture called the Office of Environmental Markets.

Keywords: Ecosystem services, landowner compensation, biodiversity, markets for ecosystem services, bundling ecosystem services, stacking ecosystem services, landowner incentives.

Introduction

One of the most challenging issues in environmental policy today is how to create incentives for private landowners to participate in conservation efforts that protect biodiversity and prevent forest and farm lands from being lost to development. No single regulation, government incentive, tax program, or other tool operates at the scale that is necessary to accomplish this goal. Biodiversity serves a number of human needs, including maintenance of ecosystem services that are critical to the sustainability of all life. Private forest and farm lands play an important role in sustaining some elements of biodiversity. One of the biggest threats to biodiversity is the loss, degradation, and fragmentation of habitat, further intensified by other worrying trends, such as climate change. These concerns also come at a time when forest and farm lands are rapidly being lost to development and conversion to other uses because economic incentives do not make it economically viable for landowners to protect these landscapes (Alig et al. 2007, Butler et al. 2004, Stein et al. 2007).

Adding to the problem, natural resource agencies are experiencing significant budget cuts, which results in cutbacks in spending for management and protection of ecosystem services. Not only is this due to the budget deficit, but also the expanding scope and severity of management problems related to climate change (Jenkins et al. 2004). The U.S. Forest Service budget is a prime example of this trend, as nearly half of that agency's budget is now used to fight fires when, just 6 years ago, only a third was used (nearly 48 percent in 2009, and 37 percent in 2004) (USDA Forest Service 2010).

Significant improvements on how we approach biodiversity conservation are needed to create better incentives for restoration and protection of ecosystems and prevent the loss of forest and farm lands to development. To help advance this goal, market-based payments for ecosystem services could be used in conjunction with other policies, such as zoning laws, tax credits, purchase of development rights, conservation easements, incentive payments, or public acquisition of lands for conservation and ecosystem protection (Bengston et al. 2004). The purpose of this paper is to explore these existing and emerging revenue streams, discuss the concepts of bundling and stacking payments as a way to promote ecological significance and economic viability, and offer policy recommendations to achieve these goals.

Ecosystem services are the benefits human communities enjoy as a result of natural processes and biological diversity. Some of these services are already recognized and sold into established markets. Timber, food, fuel and fiber are all examples of services with recognized economic value. Yet there are other services produced from healthy, functioning landscapes that are not well recognized in current payment structures, providing little or no incentive for landowners to maintain them. These services include sequestering or storing carbon in trees and soil, providing fish and wildlife habitat, filtering water, and reducing damages from natural disasters. In addition, most programs pay landowners to protect or restore a specific service rather than the suite of services produced from well-functioning ecosystems. Various incentive programs need to be better integrated or new programs need to be developed that recognize the value of ecosystem protection.

We will discuss options for bundling and stacking payments for ecosystem services to improve landowner compensation and financial viability while also delivering better ecological outcomes. Rather than being compelled to focus on one particular attribute or a discrete portion of regulated services as current programs and markets do, landowners should be able to benefit from the multiple services, both regulated and voluntary, their land is producing on a broader, landscape scale. In other words, it is important to understand the needs of an ecosystem to function well at an ecological level versus the political level. To be both ecologically and economically effective, payments, at a minimum, need to address multiple values, function at the landscape scale, and minimize transactions costs, and, to help achieve these objectives, it is critical that an integrative accounting system is developed. However the opportunities created by accessing multiple sources of revenue also raise issues that need to be addressed to ensure economic opportunities do not jeopardize ecological benefits. Previously established frameworks—ranging from how payment programs currently work to the allocation of property rights in an ecosystem services contract—will need to be reviewed and likely revamped, and development of newer policies will need to be carefully crafted.

This report will first provide an overview of existing payment programs and markets, then discuss the concepts of bundling and stacking, offer policy recommendations, and provide examples of current efforts to more effectively integrate payment opportunities for landowners.

Background

Publicly Financed Payments and Ecosystem Services

Publicly financed payments for ecosystem services can be provided in the form of a government incentive program, tax credit, or subsidy (Kroeger and Casey 2007). Although many of these payment programs were developed before the term "ecosystem services" came into common usage, they effectively pay landowners to restore and protect ecosystem services (Jack et al. 2008). The most common examples originate from the conservation title of the U.S. Farm Bill, including the

Environmental Quality Incentives Program; Conservation Stewardship Program; Wetland, Grassland and Conservation Reserve Programs; and the Conservation Reserve Enhancement Program. Although these programs are important and recognize landowners for providing ecosystem services, they currently do not encourage landscape-scale, cooperative conservation across boundaries. Instead, a field-level approach is used in which each farmer or landowner is rewarded for conservation practices conducted on a particular piece of land (Goldman et al. 2007). Participation is often opportunistic because awards are based on who gets their application in, rather than any particular strategy or goal, and not all landowners in a similar area are willing to participate. Such an approach leads to fragmentation of conservation investments scattered across the landscape. However, the Natural Resources Conservation Service is attempting to rectify this through proposing to take a watershed approach to applicant selection, focusing payments on outcomes, and prioritizing awards to landowners within certain strategic areas, such as priorities identified in State Wildlife Action Plans.

Incentive Program

The Environmental Quality Incentives Program (EQIP) under the U.S. Farm Bill is a voluntary conservation program for farmers and ranchers promoting agricultural production and environmental quality as compatible national goals (Natural Resources Conservation Service 2010). The Natural Resources Conservation Service develops contracts, up to 10 years in length, with agricultural producers to implement conservation practices that address natural resource problems. The program has broad eligibility requirements: a person must own agricultural land or be engaged in agricultural or livestock production on eligible land, which includes cropland, rangeland, pastureland, private nonindustrial forest land, and other farm and ranch lands. The program's objectives are to address impaired water quality, conserve ground and surface water resources, improve air quality, reduce soil erosion and sedimentation, and improve wildlife habitat for at-risk species. Although, effectively, EQIP pays landowners to restore or enhance ecosystem services, the program focuses on specific services and does not encourage a comprehensive landscape-level approach. Therefore, landowners are unable to recognize the economic value of other ecosystem services beyond what the program pays for.

Markets for Ecosystem Services

The term "markets for ecosystem services" refers to the market-like structures used to direct investments to landowners for improving ecosystem function. Some of these structures involve over-the-counter transactions involving one buyer and one seller, whereas others may include multiple buyers and sellers. Landowners restoring, enhancing, or protecting landscapes act as the "sellers," and buyers are the entities or individuals motivated to purchase credits for a variety of reasons, ranging from regulatory obligation to philanthropy. Market-based mechanisms provide flexibility in meeting targets, and businesses often prefer market-based regulation because it gives them options to find the most cost-effective solution to comply with environmental standards. Compliance can be obtained through production improvements to reduce pollution by purchasing credits from other firms in the regulated industry or by purchasing offset credits from approved activities that compensate for impact increases elsewhere. There is typically a range for approved activities, including natural resource conservation projects, such as planting trees or protecting a piece of land that is threatened with development.

Regulatory Markets

Policy and regulations have an important role for establishing the demand for and supply of ecosystem services, and market-based programs have developed in response to regulations for water, wetlands, and endangered species. Examples of regulation-driven markets for ecosystem services include wetland mitigation banking and water quality trading (Brauman et al. 2007, Gaddie and Regens 2000) implemented under the Clean Water Act (33 U.S.C. 1344), and species conservation banking (Carroll et al. 2007, USFWS 2003) implemented under the Endangered Species Act (16 U.S.C. 1531). A cap-and-trade approach is also being used for carbon in some countries and has successfully been used in the U.S. effort to control acid rain through limiting sulfur dioxide (SO_2) emissions (Stavins 1998, 2005). Under this program, fossil fuel electric powerplants are issued permits by the U.S. Environmental Protection Agency (EPA) for the right to generate a certain amount of SO_2 emissions. Plants that reduce their emissions below the allowance may trade their surplus allowance on an open market or auction or bank it to cover future emissions. This approach has also been developed in different regions regarding carbon emissions with the addition of natural resource project-based offsets, such as forest carbon sequestration and storage.

These existing and other emerging markets for ecosystem services offer potential financial incentives to landowners to maintain and manage forests and farm lands rather than converting to other uses. However, current legal institutions regulate and control each ecosystem service differently. Each federal and state agency with jurisdiction develops their own set of policies and regulatory frameworks, making it difficult for landowners to access ecosystem service markets and leaving gaps in the landscape. For instance, at the national level, air and water quality is regulated by the EPA, wetlands are regulated by the EPA and U.S. Army Corps of Engineers, and species conservation is controlled by the U.S. Fish and Wildlife Service (USFWS) and the National Oceanic and Atmospheric Administration. Increased agency coordination could improve the likelihood a landowner receives more than one type of payment or a larger payment, while helping to ensure payments are economically efficient and addressed in a landscape context. To provide a better understanding of each individual market, overviews of U.S. water quality trading, wetland and species mitigation banking, and carbon markets are outlined here.

Water quality trading—
Ecosystem services for water include water quality, water supply, water damage mitigation, and water-related cultural services (Brauman et al. 2007). Market-based programs for improving water quality are generally limited to local or regional programs within a specific watershed. Point sources of pollution, such as wastewater treatment facilities, typically buy credits from sellers who can either be another point source or nonpoint source, such as farmers. Sellers can generate credits for sale when they implement pollution control technologies at facilities or improve land management practices in ways that reduce water quality impacts, such as planting trees alongside streams to reduce water temperature. Forest landowners and farmers can be included as sellers of water quality credits in many programs. Other participants include water quality permitting authorities, third-party brokers, conservation organizations, watershed councils, and private industry groups. A successful example of a water quality trading program involves the EPA watershed-based permit for the Tualatin River in Oregon that allows trading to achieve the permit requirement for temperature (Cochran 2007). Here, instead of installing refrigeration systems at two Tualatin River treatment plants (at a cost of $60 million), the wastewater utility has helped pay upstream farmers to plant shade trees in the riparian areas (at a cost of $6 million). Farmers are also enrolled in the Conservation Reserve Enhancement Program, which makes it financially attractive to participate.

L. Olson

North Fork Willamette River, Oregon.

Wetland mitigation banking—
Wetland mitigation banking is one of the more robust trading programs in the country. More than 450 banks have been approved throughout the United States (U.S. EPA 2010b). Under the Clean Water Act (33 U.S.C. §1344), the U.S. Army Corps of Engineers, along with the EPA, administers a review and permitting process for the discharge of fill material in waters of the United States, including wetlands. The guiding principle is "no net loss" of wetlands. Regulated entities are required to go through a sequencing process where they must avoid or minimize wetland impacts, and, as a last resort, mitigate any damage. In this context, mitigation refers to the "restoration, establishment, enhancement, or, in certain circumstances, preservation of wetlands, streams or other aquatic resources for the purpose of offsetting unavoidable adverse impacts" (U.S. EPA 2010a). Mitigation can occur onsite, or a developer can buy credits from a landowner who established a wetland bank by creating, restoring, or enhancing a wetland. Wetland mitigation banking has developed into a well-established, market-based system where buyers and sellers of credits conduct transactions through wetland banks. Wetland ecosystems provide a broad range of ecological services demonstrably important to people including water quality and quantity, recreation, wildlife habitat, flood control, and pollution

interception (Azevedo et al. 2000, Hoehn et al. 2003). Onsite wetland mitigation has been largely unsuccessful at restoring original wetland functions, but larger offsite wetland banks are now recognized for their broader functionality and production of multiple ecosystem services (Gaddie and Regens 2000, Willamette Partnership 2010).

Wetland in Willamette Valley, Oregon.

Species conservation banking—

Species conservation banking allows the creation and trading of credits that represent wildlife conservation values on private lands. Basically, a landowner that permanently protects the natural habitat values of the land is allowed to sell credits to someone required by law to mitigate their impact to the same species and habitat on nearby land. The state of California is a leader in this area and has developed most of the conservation banks in the country; currently there are over 100 banks in existence, 94 of which are located in California (Fox and Nino-Murcia 2005).

B. Peterson

Federally endangered San Joaquin kit fox (California).

Carbon markets—

The United States is not a signatory of the Kyoto Protocol (UNFCCC 2007) nor does it have a comprehensive national policy mandating limits in carbon dioxide (CO_2) emissions. Instead, the United States has voluntary, or state and regional programs to reduce greenhouse gas (GHG) emissions. Project-based transactions can generate offset credits by an approved activity that compensates for emissions by a business in a regulated sector. Examples of offset credits include forest carbon sequestration, methane recapture, and alternative energy use. Because about 20 percent of human-induced CO_2 emissions are due to land use change and deforestation (FAO 2005), sustainable forest management can play an important role in climate change mitigation. Forestry offsets also provide a range of environmental benefits, such as wildlife habitat and water quality improvement.

Redwood forest, northern California.

Owing to the absence of a comprehensive GHG regulatory emissions reduction standard (e.g., national cap-and-trade legislation), voluntary carbon markets have dominated in the United States, and state- and regional-based programs are being developed to reduce GHG emissions. Regional and state, programs include the Regional Greenhouse Gas Initiative (RGGI) in the Northeastern United States (RGGI 2007), the Western Climate Initiative (WCI) in the Western United States (Capoor and Ambrosi 2008) and the California Climate Action Registry (CCAR 2007). However, owing to different regulatory frameworks being developed in each region and state, there is a need for the development of national standards for the registration and trading of carbon offset projects (Sampson 2004). Ruddell et al. (2007) further contend that in the absence of such national standards, forestry offset projects will continue to be limited and inconsistent.

Although the voluntary U.S. carbon market is small compared with the global carbon market (estimated at about $130 billion in 2009), the U.S. voluntary carbon market increased by 200 percent in 2007 with 13 percent of the carbon trading including carbon sequestration or forestry credits (Forestry Source 2007). By comparison, no forestry credits are accepted under the European Union Emission trading scheme, and less than 1 percent of total transactions of 430 million metric tons made under the Kyoto protocol's Clean Development Mechanism involved forestry-based credits (UNFCCC 2007). With a regulated cap-and-trade mechanism that provides higher prices than current carbon values and the allowance of forest carbon offsets, the carbon market could provide a huge incentive for forestry. However, it is important that these forestry offsets provide high-quality carbon sequestration credits to assure early investors in the carbon market that offsets are credible and provide true reductions in GHG emissions.

To address GHG policy, the forestry community has a significant opportunity to shape what kinds of forest projects are included. Lawmakers in the United States have a variety of legislation and pending legislation with significant implications for carbon and forestry including the 2008 Farm Bill, 2009 American Clean Energy and Security Waxman-Markey bill, and other federal and state legislation. Two key components for any forestry offset projects include keeping forest land in forests, and increasing carbon sequestration through forest management while ensuring that it is not at the expense of other ecological values, such as biodiversity. There are also a number of important policy issues to incorporate in forestry offsets, including clear definitions for carbon baselines and additionality, permanence and leakage, possible inclusion of wood products for the long-term storage of carbon, and projects that promote additional carbon sequestration and discourage conversion of forests to other land uses (Cathcart 2000, Ruddell et al. 2007).

Voluntary Markets

Voluntary markets can act as another tool to help motivate landowners to engage in resource restoration and conservation activities, and, absent regulatory reform, help to fill the gaps in the current regulatory structure. Over the last few years, international collaborators ranging from oil and gas companies, the United Nations, and conservation groups have been working together to develop a voluntary market, the Business and Biodiversity Offsets Program, to make biodiversity offsets "…a standard part of business practice for those companies with a significant impact on biodiversity" (BBOP 2010). Businesses are encouraged to use offsets to compensate for the residual impact to biodiversity that cannot be avoided or mitigated onsite and more properly balance impacts from a project. Developers are only encouraged to use offsets after they have applied the mitigation hierarchy in which the first priority is for a developer to avoid an impact altogether, then minimize it as much as possible, and, finally, turn to mitigation if an impact cannot effectively be avoided or minimized.

In addition, Defenders of Wildlife, along with partners in the public and private sector, initiated a project called the Marketplace for Nature (Defenders of Wildlife

2010). Its purpose is to highlight proposed or partially completed conservation projects that have ecosystem service credits for sale in regulated or voluntary markets. An online tool developed by Defenders, called the Conservation Registry (www. conservationregistry.org), will include a page dedicated to the Marketplace for Nature, making information about the projects easy to find. Part of the work associated with this effort includes development of a habitat metric that can help promote voluntary restoration and conservation of unregulated habitats. The overall goal is to create a metric with a national framework that can be implemented locally. The framework provides a standard approach to measuring habitat quality and includes determining the indicators for a particular vegetation type or ecosystem; the key ecological processes (such as fire and flooding) to maintain the site; the current condition of the site; the social and ecological context of the site (size of the site, proximity to identified conservation priorities, and surrounding land uses); and the site's management security (ownership, easements, and agreements) (Defenders of Wildlife 2010). The project will initially apply these standards to a few selected habitats to ensure that it provides an effective valuation and can be replicated across different habitat types. The calculators for the selected habitats will be posted on the Marketplace for Nature page in the Conservation Registry so landowners can easily access them.

The lack of demand or regulatory driver for voluntary markets generates skepticism as to whether voluntary approaches can legitimately improve ecological conditions (Bayon et al. 2007). To help address this issue, the Business for Biodiversity Program and Marketplace for Nature project are taking theory and applying it on the ground. These real-world applications can help inform the debate on the effectiveness of voluntary markets and provide the opportunity to evaluate and reevaluate how practices and policies can be improved to contribute to better ecological and economic outcomes. On-the-ground experience can provide important lessons and will be important to demonstrate the strengths and weaknesses of voluntary market approaches.

Voluntary Actions and Agreements

Businesses are under increasing pressure to ensure that their practices and investments are socially and environmentally responsible. Different types of "green investments" have emerged that offer opportunities for businesses to demonstrate commitment toward sustainable development and practices. With the development of carbon policies and markets, many companies have taken notice of the size of their carbon footprints; the rise of other, more integrated ecosystem markets could similarly lead to companies recognizing the extent of their environmental impact.

If companies begin to acknowledge and account for their ecological footprint, they may be interested in investing in restoration or conservation projects that support ecosystem services. These investments could help a company to obtain some type of "label" or "certification" similar to the Leadership in Energy and Environmental Design certification for buildings (USGBC 2010). This becomes a branding tool for business and allows consumers the opportunity to purchase products that are produced in a way that contributes to ecosystem restoration or conservation efforts.

Other entities, both public and private, have already begun to voluntarily contract with landowners for ecosystem services. These contracts or agreements often occur when transaction costs make it unlikely that private landowners will take the initiative to act, as in cases involving numerous small landholders, or when private parties lack the necessary authority for implementing plans. A common voluntary agreement used to protect land from development is a conservation easement which, in effect, protects ecosystem services provided by the protected land. A landowner gives up a right (or rights) associated with their property, usually related to development (Land Trust Alliance 2010). The landowner can donate the easement, or an organization or agency can purchase it. The easement holder is often the purchaser or designated third party and is responsible for ensuring the easement's integrity in perpetuity. Landowners who donate conservation easements that meet federal tax code regulations can be eligible for a tax deduction equal to the difference in fair market value of the property before and after the easement takes effect (Land Trust Alliance 2010).

There are also examples of businesses that rely on a particular ecosystem service that contributes to the production of a marketable product, and, as a result, provide financial incentives to landowners to improve land management practices. For example, Perrier Vittel (now Nestlé Waters) encouraged landowners to adopt improved agricultural practices and reforest sensitive infiltration zones to protect the water supply used for Perrier's bottled mineral water (Perrot-Maître and Davis 2001). The company invested just over $9 million to buy approximately 1500 ha of farmland, and some of these acquired lands were rented back to farmers who were willing to improve their management practices (Perrot-Maître 2001). The company also signed 18- to 30-year contracts with farmers who agreed to switch to less intensive dairy farming and pasture management (Perrot-Maître 2001). These agreements cover about 40 farms consisting of over 10 000 ha of farmland (Perrot-Maître 2001). Farmers are compensated for the risk and reduced profitability associated with the transition, with the company paying them $230 per hectare per year for 7 years (Perrot-Maître 2001).

Discussion

Bundling and Stacking: Frameworks to Integrate Payments

Optimizing multiple ecosystem service values can prevent maximization of one value at the expense of another and create a greater amount of ecological improvement for a site than if the focus is on one particular ecosystem service. In fact, failing to recognize the interconnectedness among ecosystem services on a landscape can lead to their degradation, as emphasis on one ecosystem service could undermine the provision of another (Salzman et al. 2001). Studies have shown that increasing the provision of one ecosystem service does not necessarily increase the provision of another (Nelson et al. 2008). For example, planting Douglas-fir trees (*Pseudotsuga menziesii* (Mirb.) Franco) in a native prairie in the Pacific Northwest could have a significant carbon sequestration benefit, but could also be detrimental to native biodiversity values. However, the concepts of bundling and stacking ecosystem services payments can promote the integration of multiple ecological values, providing a more holistic view of natural systems and greater ecological benefits than a single-program or market approach.

"Bundling" ecosystem services refers to merging multiple ecological values from a piece of property under a single credit type. For example, if a landowner restores a hectare of riparian forest, it results in improvements to more than one ecosystem service, including reducing stream temperature, improving wildlife habitat, sequestering carbon, and mitigating damage from potential floods. Bundling, as defined, would allow these services to be sold under a single credit type—e.g., an ecosystem service credit. Bundling might provide a way for landowners to get paid for the broader benefits they are providing, while also giving buyers flexibility in meeting regulatory needs or voluntary investments. Whether or not this type of credit could be sold into a regulatory market, however, will depend on agency rules, but it is unlikely that it would happen anytime in the near future considering how natural resources are regulated. Ideally, an integrative accounting system would "bundle" ecosystem services at a landscape scale and accommodate current jurisdictional limitations by separating out regulated credits and "stacking" them alongside other parts of the bundled services.

"Stacking" is a concept closely related to bundling. There can be variations on how stacking might work, but, generally, stacking ecosystem services can allow landowners to independently sell different types of credits from a single piece of property by using multiple market-based strategies. For each credit type, the applicable market rules will apply. For example, if a landowner restores a single hectare of riparian forest, it could produce water quality credits, carbon credits, riparian habitat credits, and conservation banking credits that the landowner could sell into each respective market. Whereas a bundled credit is a bunch of services grouped together from the same acre of land under a single credit type, stacked credits are generated from the same acre of land, but accounted for and sold separately into each market structure. Stacking can potentially accommodate regulatory and voluntary market structures.

The concept of "stacking," however, is not necessarily limited to selling multiple types of credits within regulated or voluntary markets. Landowners can also stack different types of payments, including payments from market-based programs, as well as government incentive programs and voluntary agreements. For example, a landowner might receive a grant from a state agency to do a prairie restoration project, but might also be eligible to sell habitat credits from an upland portion of the site, while also receiving a tax credit for placing a conservation easement on the entire property. This landowner has effectively accessed or stacked multiple sources of revenue for the benefits provided through restoration and conservation activities.

Costa Rica: Pago por Servicios Ambientales—

One of the most successful programs demonstrating stacking payments is the Pago por Servicios Ambientales (payment for environmental services) program in Costa Rica* which reduces carbon dioxide emissions through a tax on burning fossil fuels (Salzman 2005). Since the 1960s, Costa Rica has had one of the highest deforestation rates in the world. To address this issue, the government established goals for protecting remaining primary forest, encouraging regrowth of secondary forest, and promoting tree plantations on degraded soils to meet demands for timber and paper. Specifically, the government amended its Forestry Law to allow landowners to be compensated for the "environmental services" produced from their lands. The government contracts with landowners to provide services, namely watershed protection, carbon sequestration and storage, protection of biodiversity resources, and protection of key life zones.

The landowners relinquish these ecosystem service rights for the contract period, giving the government the ability to sell carbon offsets and watershed protection to domestic and international buyers (USDA Forest Service 2007).

To make it more financially attractive for landowners to participate and achieve the necessary level of protection needed to reverse the deforestation trend, the Costa Rican government decided to look beyond the national sales tax to fund the program. The government generates additional funding through contracts with pharmaceutical companies for biodiversity prospecting, agreements with hydropower producers in Costa Rica, and joint carbon sequestration implementation projects (Salzman 2005). Therefore, many different sources of revenues are "stacked" to deliver a higher payment. Landowners receive an average annual payment of about $32 per hectare to participate in the program; payments have ranged from $22 per hectare to $42 per hectare (Sánchez-Azofeifa et al. 2007). This exceeds current rents for active pasture, which would be the alternative choice for landowners. Depending on location, cattle ranching earns landowners between $20 and $30 per hectare (Sánchez-Azofeifa et al. 2007). There was initial concern that few landowners would volunteer to participate. However, within a short time, the program was over-subscribed, and new sources of funding are being explored to expand it (Pagiola 2007).

---

*Another successful payment program for ecosystem services is in Brazil where the government charges a fee to resource users which is then pooled in a fund to pay landowners to restore and protect ecosystem services.

Both bundling and stacking effectively provide landowners with an opportunity to access multiple sources of revenue. Ideally, this will promote greater economic incentive for landowner participation and, in turn, greater ecological benefits because more landowners will be engaging in conservation on a broader, landscape scale. In addition, since agencies are not typically encouraged to work beyond their specific mandates, bundling and stacking give them the opportunity to coordinate and address issues beyond typical jurisdictions. Working across these arbitrary lines can help break the cycle of agencies operating in silos, encourage integrated management that transcends arbitrary boundaries, and provide support for more comprehensive management of ecosystem services. Yet the policy decisions that will be made around whether ecosystem markets should be developing bundled, unbundled, or stacked credits are constrained in the short term by the realities of market development and government regulation (Halsey 2009). Current markets are developing credit measures that are a discrete, unbundled selection of natural functions. This is a direct reflection of the narrow legislative mandates that created the regulations in the first place (Halsey 2009). There are risks in furthering this fragmented approach because it fails to provide the financial incentives needed to encourage landowners to conserve multiple ecosystem services.

If separate processes are used to account for different types of regulated credits, but stacking is allowed, it is still an imperfect step because it misses the unregulated parts of nature (Halsey 2009). Although stacking in this sense represents a step in the right direction because it broadens the consideration of a site's values to more than one ecosystem service, it is not promoting an integrated approach and makes it very difficult to understand the ecological improvements on a landscape level. Bundling, on the other hand, represents an integrated ecosystem approach because it can evaluate a parcel as a whole and measure overall increase of both regulated and unregulated ecological values whereas stacking immediately separates a parcel into its discrete pieces—one without regard to the other—based on what the market dictates and regardless of the needs of the ecosystem. Preferably, an accounting tool would measure overall improvements in ecosystem functions and allow regulated credits to be unbundled and stacked, while allowing for the unregulated services to be sold as one overarching ecosystem or habitat credit. Such a combined accounting approach promotes the needs of the ecosystem and recognizes existing regulatory frameworks. In the meantime, until an accounting tool is developed that agencies feel comfortable using to account for regulated mandates, unregulated values could be bundled under a single credit type and stacked to be sold along with other regulated credits from the same piece of land.

In reality, accommodating current legal mandates will be easier and quicker than overhauling the way resources are regulated, particularly considering that many of the laws regulating the environment have been in place for nearly 40 years. Voluntary markets, however, do offer the opportunity to bundle resources without being constrained by the regulatory market structure. Concerns do arise over whether there will be enough demand in a voluntary market to get to scale, but the rise of carbon offset markets provides good insight as to how individuals, communities, and businesses are increasingly interested in trying to alleviate some of their impact on the environment. Similarly, buyers—whether it's a business that wants to invest in environmentally responsible projects or an individual seeking to protect habitat values in their community—could purchase a bundled credit to voluntarily mitigate their whole ecological footprint, not just their carbon footprint.

Still, regardless of whether a payment or credit is stacked or bundled, there are many policy issues that need to be addressed to ensure that what is being done on-the-ground is actually improving rather than diminishing overall ecological health. In fact, there are some critical issues that need to be addressed to help markets and payments for ecosystem services develop in a manner that is both good for the environment and financially viable for landowner participation.

Policy Issues

Defining property rights and ecosystem services—

Most ecosystem services have public good characteristics and, therefore, present complex allocation questions in the private property rights context. A basic foundation of property law is that owning land comes with a "bundle of sticks," each corresponding to a particular right or duty, primary among them the right to occupy the land, to exclude others, and to decide whether or not to develop the land (Carroll et al. 2007). One of the primary questions is how markets for ecosystem services affect this established area of law (Patterson and Coelho 2009). Does it require defining new rights and duties or redefining old ones (Ruhl et al. 2007)? Defining new rights can be particularly difficult because to fully account for all the relevant property interests, rights should be assigned to the supplier of the ecosystem service, as well as determining from which properties the service flows (Ruhl et al. 2007). Rights would need to be distributed among multiple landowners, making universal agreement and enforcement particularly complicated (Ruhl et al. 2007).

Yet another perspective is that property rights may not be poorly defined, but need to be redefined because, historically, property law has given landowners complete discretion with strong incentives to develop, rather than protect, ecosystem services (Ruhl et al. 2007). Property law often reflects contemporary social and political values, and land has typically been considered more valuable if it was in production or developable. However, values can change. Wetlands represent a prime example of this evolution (Ruhl et al. 2007). In the past, wetlands were viewed as bacteria-producing, mosquito-infested wastelands that should be developed and drained for public health purposes. Over time, however, society began to realize the benefits wetlands provided, and a shift in thinking started to occur, eventually resulting in mandated wetlands protection under the Clean Water Act.

Current market-based programs demonstrate different approaches to assigning property rights. For example, the Clean Water Act limits private property rights for wetlands in a way that is aimed at protecting the public interest in wetlands (Kroeger and Casey 2007). The law creates a public policy allowing for "no net loss of wetlands," and, as a result, impacts to wetlands must be avoided, minimized, or mitigated. Agency guidelines allow mitigation banking as a way to offset unavoidable wetland impacts, thereby providing a right for landowners with wetlands on their property to create, restore, or enhance wetlands and sell credits generated from these activities to regulated entities. Other examples demonstrate a different approach when services flow beyond a property's boundaries. The Clean Water Services' project on the Tualatin River in Oregon, where a wastewater utility pays landowners for planting trees along streams in the watershed rather than investing in a cooling tower, represents an example of a collective-right approach. The property right of land ownership makes the ecosystem service private and landowner modification of land management practices supplies the desired ecosystem service (cooler water). A collective-right structure is essentially created where these rights are aggregated or bundled among landowners and, by paying their bill, the service of cleaning wastewater is essentially "sold" to the rate payers who are benefiting from it (Duraiappah 2006). This type of approach, however, typically relies on the cooperation of many landowners to achieve the desired ecological results, which could be difficult in some circumstances.

Assuming rights in ecosystem services are assigned to the provider or landowner, the concepts of bundling and stacking even further complicate the notion of property rights, particularly when public money is used to fund a restoration or conservation project. For example, if a local government program pays a landowner to plant native trees along a riparian corridor, does the government now own any available ecosystem service credits? Or does the landowner? Or does each retain a portion of the total credits? Is the taxpayer paying twice for the same service? A couple of options may exist. If the government were to retain the right to the credit, then the revenue generated from the credit sales could be applied to the program's budget that provided the original funding for the landowner. It would essentially work as a revolving fund. Revenue beyond what was originally funded to the landowner could either go to the same landowner for supplemental activities, or it could lead to opportunities for other landowners to participate. Another option may be to give the landowner the right to the credit regardless of the source of capital, thereby eliminating the government's role entirely and increasing landowner incentives for restoration and conservation. If public money generated the outcomes, however, there is an argument that the public (taxpayer) should benefit, not the landowner. Currently, there is no clear answer on the best way to approach these complex issues, but it will be important to try to strike an appropriate balance between individual property rights while preventing abuse from the public sector (Duraiappah 2006). Because the most appropriate type of market-based approach will differ among ecosystem services, it is also likely property-rights allocations will differ, as current programs have demonstrated (Kroeger and Casey 2007).

Conservation easements present another property law conundrum. Not only is there a question of who owns the rights to ecosystem services—the easement holder or the landowner—but also how markets for ecosystem services will affect property appraisals. Appraisals are based on traditional methodologies that consider only the loss of value associated with the easement's restrictions on land use and management, including agricultural and development potential (Taylor 2010). Because market values for ecosystem services are not well established or even recognized in many cases, the economic values of these services are not considered in the easement valuation (Taylor 2010). However, carbon markets could provide a real opportunity for landowners, especially if a cap-and-trade system is put in place. This will likely require appraisers to take carbon credit values into consideration and would significantly affect the value of an easement and potentially the tax benefits. The same issue will arise as other ecosystem service markets develop.

Regarding credit ownership, for market-based programs that require a conservation easement as a condition of the program, the landowner holds the right to sell the credits. Under species conservation banking, landowners need to permanently protect the land they are preserving for habitat so the right to sell the credits stays with the landowner. Where the issue becomes difficult is when an easement is not required or an easement is placed on a property without recognition of the potential market-based opportunities. A few options exist: it could be a universal rule that landowners own the right to sell all ecosystem service credits generated on their property; rights could be determined by who is actually funding the restoration or maintenance work on the property, so if it's the easement holder, then they hold the right to sell ecosystem services and vice versa; or it could be negotiated in the easement contract to either the landowner or the easement holder.

U.S. Wetlands Reserve Program—

The Wetlands Reserve Program offers technical assistance and financial support to landowners for protecting, restoring, and enhancing wetlands on their property. The Natural Resources Conservation Service administers this program, and the overall goal is to "achieve the greatest wetlands functions and values, along with optimum wildlife habitat, on every acre enrolled in the program" (USDA Natural Resources Conservation Service 2010). In other words, the program focuses on improving the ecosystem services wetlands provide, including fish and wildlife habitat, water quality, and flood control. Landowners are compensated through payments for conservation easements based on the fair market value of the property rights covered by the easement. Ecosystem service values are not considered in the easement valuation, nor are participating landowners given incentive to look beyond the wetland to evaluate how other practices or actions on other areas affect the wetland and other ecosystem services. More recently, studies have emerged documenting the potential for wetlands to sequester carbon and questioning whether this can be valued. If so, landowners might be able to sell carbon credits from wetland projects, raising another issue: would the easement holder or landowner have the right to sell these credits? It could be argued that since the government paid for the easement protecting the wetland, then the government owns the right to sell the credits. Yet, if the landowner does additional restoration work that facilitates carbon sequestration, it can be argued that the right to sell the carbon credits belongs to the landowner. So far, current policies do not allow landowners to sell wetland mitigation banking credits from wetlands restored with public funds, unless additional activities occur beyond what was paid for with the public funds, and, so far, carbon markets have been designed around the same caliber, requiring natural resource offset projects to provide "additional" benefits.

Mixing public financing and markets (or double dipping)—
Because stacking payments can include mixing public funds with for-profit endeavors, one of the biggest policy concerns is to ensure that the same values are not being sold more than once. This issue is intimately related to the debate on what should be considered "additional," or in other words above baseline, and, therefore, creditable or payable. Additionality is the notion that a project must reduce impacts beyond what would have occurred in the absence of the project (UNFCCC 2010). The concern is, if a landowner is compensated for one action, then accumulates a second, third, or fourth payment, it could potentially cost more for the same outcome. For example, if a landowner receives federal funds to restore a wetland through the U.S. Department of Agriculture's Conservation Reserve Program or the U.S. Fish and Wildlife Service's Partners for Fish and Wildlife Program, the U.S. Environmental Protection Agency, Army Corps of Engineers, and the U.S. Fish and Wildlife Service do not allow the landowner to turn around and sell credits into a compensatory market (40 CFR Part 230, 19676, April 10, 2008; USFWS Guidance). A landowner can only do so if they conduct activities that are supplemental to what the federal funding paid for.

Policies could continue to follow the Corps, EPA and U.S. Fish and Wildlife Service approach. Or, another option might be to simply prohibit co-mingling or stacking of public and private funds. However, the reality is there isn't always enough money in current programs (public payments, tax subsidies, etc.) to finance the restoration and conservation work that needs to be done, so landowners will likely need to access various sources of capital. On the other hand, if regulatory mitigation or offset programs are established to "offset" the impacts of a development activity, there is a need to ensure that a landowner's on-the-ground actions are actually producing the offset. In addition, preventing the use of mixed-revenue sources might continue to promote the status quo of a single-resource approach rather than figuring out how programs can be better integrated and more efficient.

An alternative approach might be to allow credits that can be generated from a federally funded project to act as match or cost share (Parsons 2009). Most federal funding programs require matching funds as a condition of a grant, and current economic conditions can make compliance difficult. Federally funded habitat restoration and conservation projects could generate marketable credits, such as sequestered or stored carbon, that could be counted toward overall project funding. To help alleviate concerns about co-mingling revenue sources or double dipping, contracts could require that any revenue received from credit sales be used to further the goals of the project, ranging from site maintenance, additional restoration work, or adjacent land acquisitions.

Still another option may be to universally allow credit sales, regardless of revenue source. If a landowner receives a payment to restore a wetland or plant trees, the landowner could still be eligible to sell wetlands credits and forest carbon offsets. If the ultimate goal is to get more landowners to engage in conservation, then giving them access to multiple sources of financing—without strings attached—might make it more economically viable for them. Yet, it could compromise ecological benefits because the same values could be bought and sold many times.

The optimal solution may lie somewhere in the middle of these options, but it will be important for any policies developed to promote balance among ecological integrity, administrative efficiency, equity, and economic efficiency and sustainability.

Understanding the role of government—
Government has an integral role to play in further developing incentive programs and creating demand for market-based actions through regulation. Government will also have a critical role in developing market standards and providing technical expertise for implementation. However, the limits of government participation as a seller of ecosystem services have not been clearly defined.

For example, there is support for allowing the U.S. Forest Service to sell forest carbon credits or offer offsets from stored and sequestered carbon on national forests. In fact, the National Forest Foundation created the Carbon Capital Fund as a way for private donors to offset their personal carbon emissions through making financial contributions for reforestation projects on national forests (National Forest

Foundation 2010). Yet, this approach could be perceived as risky because, although it could potentially provide the Forest Service with an alternate revenue source, credits or offsets generated from national forests might flood the market and discourage private landowner participation. If the biggest threat to forests is deforestation on private lands, then incentives and market-based opportunities need to work for private landowners. In addition, because the Forest Service is already tasked with maintaining and protecting national forests with taxpayer dollars, sequestration benefits might not be considered truly "additional" and Congress might simply slash the Forest Service budget if credits can be sold from national forests, making it very difficult to secure funding for these public lands.

State government, however, might play a different role than the federal government in their ability to sell credits. There are state land-management agencies specifically tasked with generating revenue for the benefit of schools or other state needs. Typically, state land management agencies are faced with selling land for development, and some state agencies, like the Oregon Department of State Lands, have begun to explore selling ecosystem services credits. The opportunity to sell credits into multiple ecosystem services markets not only could generate revenue for the state, but also provide better ecological results.

Overall, the primary concerns to address in developing policies around the role of government in selling credits are to ensure there is room for private landowners to participate, public lands are not compromised, and the natural environment is better off than it otherwise would have been.

Regional Examples of Making Payments and Markets Work Together

There are emerging efforts trying to address some of the policy issues discussed above, and some are even testing tools to value ecosystem services and associated policies on the ground.

Oregon Senate Bill 513 (ecosystem markets legislation)—
Oregon is one of the first states to pass legislation addressing the importance of ecosystem markets and encouraging the development of coordinated and efficient markets for ecosystem services in the state. The basic premise behind the bill is that without a coordinated approach, small, random markets will emerge and fade away without producing tangible ecological or economic benefits. Without a coherent overall policy, markets for some services could stimulate investment in activities with other adverse social or ecological impacts while public agencies and industries with regulatory obligations will continue to face expensive delays and end up investing in projects with marginal benefits. If a marketplace is carefully structured,

however, it can provide revenue to landowners who provide ecosystem services, expedite development projects, and produce much greater environmental benefits than the current fragmented approach. Specifically, the bill acknowledges the importance of ecosystem services; establishes a state policy to support the maintenance, enhancement, and restoration of ecosystem services throughout the state; and forms a working group to address some of the more complex legal and policy issues associated with creating and coordinating market-based programs. The working group is charged with making recommendations to the 2011 legislature.

Counting on the Environment (Willamette Partnership)—
The Willamette Partnership is a coalition of public and private sector leaders working to build an integrated ecosystem services marketplace in Oregon. The partnership has made significant progress in securing regulatory approval for credit accounting procedures and policies that support the effective and credible implementation of ecosystem services. The partnership received a U.S. Department of Agriculture Conservation Innovation Grant to develop an accounting tool that could generate multiple credits. So far, the project, called "Counting on the Environment," has secured regulatory approval in Oregon to pilot test the multiple credit accounting tool, which calculates wetland, water quality (related to temperature), salmonid habitat, and prairie credits (Willamette Partnership 2010). Although the accounting tool primarily uses other approved regulatory tools as a basis and focuses on regulated markets, the prairie calculator is unique because no regulated market exists for prairie habitat credits. The calculator is calibrated toward an endangered prairie species—Fenders' blue butterfly (*Icaricia icarioides fenderi*)—but is primarily intended to quantify the habitat values produced from a properly functioning prairie in the Willamette Valley.

The Counting on the Environment project also developed an approach to selling stacked credits, that is currently being tested. The partnership allows credits to be stacked from a single geographic "unit" within a property's boundary, but for each credit, the applicable, separate tool will be used to calculate the credits. If any credits are sold, the proportionate percentage needs to be subtracted from the other credits available for sale. For example, a riparian unit defined within a property's boundaries could sell wetland, water quality, and salmon credits. Each crediting tool would be applied to the unit to produce the number of credits available for sale. As each credit is based on a different currency, there will be variations. Therefore, a restoration activity might produce 10 wetland credits (based on acres), 100 salmon credits (based on linear feet), and a million water temperature credits (based on kilocalories per day). If 50 out of the 100 salmon credits were sold, which is the equivalent of 50 percent, then both the wetlands and water temperature credits would need to be reduced by 50 percent, leaving 5 wetland credits and 500,000 water temperature credits to be sold (along with 50 remaining salmon credits).

To avoid the thorny issue of mixing publicly financed projects with market-based revenues, the partnership chose projects that currently do not have public financing attached to them. Because many of the agencies have not come up with a common approach, the partnership decided not to take the risk and potentially jeopardize funding opportunities for landowners. As policies become established, the partnership plans to revisit this issue.

The Bay Bank—
Private landowners own the majority of the land in the Chesapeake Bay watershed and, as a result, the future health of the bay and its watershed depends greatly on their actions. The Bay Bank was formed to address the need to reduce the amount of phosphorus and nitrogen entering the Chesapeake Bay from multiple states and find ways to facilitate farm and forest landowner access to multiple revenue sources, including voluntary and regulatory ecosystem markets and conservation programs, through an easy-to-use online marketplace (Bay Bank 2010, Pinchot Institute 2010). The Bay Bank focuses on carbon sequestration, habitat conservation, water quality, and forest protection.

The Bay Bank approaches stacking differently than the Willamette Partnership, primarily because it solely credits actions (versus outcomes). If market rules allow for stacking, and it can be shown that the individual actions generating credits for stacking are additional, the Bay Bank will accept the credits (Lien 2010). Therefore, stacked credits will be accepted if two discrete conservation actions on the same piece of property can be shown to generate multiple benefits that are not captured in a single credit type. The Bay Bank, however, will not accept stacked credits generated from a single conservation action. For example, if a landowner agrees to maintain a forest stand rather than sell it for a new housing development and then separately agrees to manage the forest to produce and maintain a specific habitat type, these are two different creditable conservation actions: the forest bank requires preventing conversion of the forest, which is one action, and habitat maintenance requires certain land management activities, which is perceived as an additional action.

With respect to bundling, the Bay Bank is supportive of the development of bundled credit types in voluntary market spaces. In fact, the Bay Bank is currently developing voluntary habitat market protocols, and credits resulting from these protocols will essentially be bundled. The Bay Bank will accept bundled credits in regulated markets as regulatory agencies provide relevant policy guidance.

U.S. Department of Agriculture, Office of Environmental Markets—
Congress passed the 2008 U.S. Farm Bill with a provision in the conservation
title addressing markets for ecosystem services.[1] An interagency "Conservation
and Land Management Environmental Services Board" was created to assist the
Secretary of Agriculture in developing the technical guidelines that the federal government will use to assess ecosystem services provided by conservation and land
management activities.[2] The Office of Environmental Markets was also established
to provide the administrative and technical support to the Secretary of Agriculture
in implementing this provision.

This new office aims to facilitate interagency coordination on the topic of
ecosystem services and markets while also ensuring collaboration with other entities, like the Willamette Partnership and Bay Bank. A real concern associated with
the emergence of ecosystem markets and the enthusiasm surrounding them is that
many players will start entering the game and make separate rules for each market.
The Office of Environmental Markets is in the best position to help alleviate this
concern. The new director, Sally Collins, sees the office's critical role as facilitat-
ing interagency consultation and leveraging expertise across government to ensure
consistency in standards and protocol development and to move toward a unified
system for registration and verification to help the government operate as one
(National Association of State Foresters 2009) (emphasis added).

Aside from coordinating with existing efforts like the Willamette Partnership
and the Bay Bank, the agency will likely make recommendations and offer consis-
tent guidelines as some of the bigger policy issues get tested on the ground. Overall,
the creation of this agency represents a commitment by the federal government to
develop market-based opportunities for landowners and learn from existing efforts
in this field while helping to organize these efforts to create efficiencies.

---

[1] Section 2709 of the 2008 U.S. Farm Bill directs the Secretary of Agriculture to establish
technical guidelines that outline science-based methods for measuring environmental
benefits from conservation. The purpose is to help build a more unified, transparent market
system where landowners can participate in emerging markets, and investors trust that they
are purchasing a real conservation benefit.

[2] Environmental Services Board members include the Secretaries of the Interior, Energy,
Commerce, Transportation; the Assistant Secretary of the Army, Civil Works; the Chair-
man of the Council of Economic Advisors; the Director of the Office of Science and
Technology Policy; the Administrator of the Environmental Protection Agency; and the
Assistant Deputy Under Secretary of Defense for Environment, Safety and Occupational
Health. The Secretary of Agriculture is chair of the Board; the Chairman of Council on
Environmental Quality and the Administrator of the Office of Information and Regulatory
Affairs, Office of Management and Budget, are vice-chairs.

Conclusion

Because of the threats to biodiversity and the further escalating environmental problems related to climate change, now, more than ever, additional economic incentives are needed for landowners to engage in restoration and protection of ecosystem services. In addition, because forest and farm lands provide an important role in sustaining some parts of biodiversity, it is critical that better economic incentives are created for landowners to help prevent the loss of these lands to development. Payments focused on ecosystem services potentially provide promising opportunities for landowners, particularly if landowners can access or stack multiple sources of revenue. If correctly implemented, bundling or stacking policies could promote landscape-scale conservation and help move financial incentives toward a more holistic approach of protecting ecosystems.

However, this is not an easy task. Many established legal and policy frameworks associated with regulation of the natural environment have been in place for nearly 40 years, and it requires a shift in thinking on how to approach environmental problems. In addition, policy issues have not been thoroughly vetted, and there is a very real concern that markets might prove to be financially viable but not ecologically significant or, possibly, even damaging. It is critical that, as these markets develop, the goals and policies developed take into account the bigger picture and do not set expectations on short-sighted economic returns. The current efforts described here, that are working to ensure the ecological integrity of programs based on ecosystem services and testing concepts on the ground, will provide valuable information on how to make programs effective.

Metric Equivalents

When you know:	Multiply by:	To get:
Hectares (ha)	2.47	Acres
Kilograms (kg)	2.205	Tons

References

Alig, R.J. 2007. A United States view on changes in land use and land values affecting sustainable forest management. In: Deal, R.L.; White, R.; Benson, G., eds. Emerging issues for sustainable forest management. Journal of Sustainable Forestry. 24(2/3): 209–228.

Azevedo, C.D.; Heriges, J.A.; King, C.L. 2000. Iowa wetlands: perceptions of values. Ames, IA: Iowa State University, Center for Agricultural and Rural Development. 30 p.

Bay Bank, 2010. About the Bay Bank. http://www.thebaybank.org/. (June 4, 2010).

Bayon, R. 2007. Voluntary carbon markets. London: Earthscan Publications: 13–16.

Bengston, D.N.; Fletcher, J.O.; Nelson, K.C. 2004. Public policies for managing urban growth and protecting open space: policy instruments and lessons learned in the United States. Landscape and Urban Planning. 69: 271–286.

Brauman, K.A.; Daily, G.C.; Duarte, T.; Mooney, H.A. 2007. The nature and value of ecosystem services: an overview highlighting hydrologic services. Annual Review of Environment and Resources. 32: 67–98.

Business and Biodiversity Offsets Program [BBOP], 2010. http://bbop.forest-trends.org/index.php. (April 14, 2010).

Butler, B.; Swenson, J.; Alig, R. 2004. Forest fragmentation in the Pacific Northwest: quantifications and correlations. Forest Ecology and Management. 189: 363–373.

California Climate Action Registry [CCAR]. 2007. Forest sector protocol. Version 2.1. September. 68 p. http://www.climateregistry.org/resources/docs/protocols/industry/forest/forest_sector_protocol_version_2.1_sept2007.pdf. (February 17, 2010).

Capoor, K.; Ambrosi, P. 2008. State and trends of the carbon market 2008. Washington, DC: World Bank Institute. 71 p.

Carroll, N.; Fox, J.; Bayon, R., eds. 2007. Conservation and biodiversity banking: a guide to setting up and running biodiversity credit trading systems. London: Earthscan Publications. 7–73 p.

Cathcart, J.F. 2000. Forests, carbon, and climate change. Journal of Forestry. 98(9): 32–37.

Clean Water Act (CWA), 1977. 33 U.S.C. 1344.

Cochran, B. 2007. Can markets deliver water quality? Western Forester. 52(2): 6–7.

Collins, S. 2009. National Association of State Forests [NASF]. Annual meeting. Developing markets for ecosystem services. http://www.stateforesters.org/files/ Collins-2009-NASF.pdf.

Collins, S.; Larry, B. 2008. Caring for our natural assets: an ecosystems services perspective. In: Deal, R.L., ed. Integrated restoration of forested ecosystems to achieve multi-resource benefits. Proceedings of the 2007 national silviculture workshop. Gen. Tech. Rep. PNW-GTR-733. Portland, OR: U.S. Department of Agriculture, Forest Service, Pacific Northwest Research Station: 1–11.

Defenders of Wildlife, 2010. Marketplace for nature. http://www.defenders.org/ programs_and_policy/biodiversity_partners/ecosystem_marketplace/mfn/index. php. (May 27, 2010).

Duraiappah, A. 2006. Markets for ecosystem services: a potential tool for multilateral environmental agreements. http://www.iisd.org/pdf/2007/economcs_ markets_eco_services.pdf. (April 14, 2010).

Endangered Species Act (ESA), 1973. 16 U.S.C. 1531–1536, 1538–1540.

Food and Agricultural Organization [FAO]. 2005. Global forest resources assessment 2005—progress towards sustainable forest management. FAO Forestry Paper 147. Rome: Food and Agriculture Organization of the United Nations. 320 p.

Forestry Source. 2007. Carbon credit quality, price key to carbon markets. The Forestry Source. 12(9): 1–2.

Fox, J.; Nino-Murcia, A. 2005. Status of species conservation banking in the United States. Conservation Biology. 19(4): 996–1007.

Gaddie, R.K.; Regens, J.L. 2000. Regulating wetlands protection: environmental federalism and the states. In: Kraft, M.E.; Wilson, H., eds. SUNY series in environmental politics and policy. Albany, NY: State University of New York Press: 1–10.

Goldman, R.; Thompson, B.; Daily, G. 2007. Managing U.S. agricultural lands for ecosystem services. http://woods.stanford.edu/docs/farmbill/Managing_US_Agricultural_Lands_for_Ecosystem_Services.pdf. (April 14, 2010).

Halsey, K. 2009. Bundling of ecosystem service credits. Oregon State University panel presentation. On file with: http://people.oregonstate.edu/groups/biodiversity/Ecosysbundling.html.

Hoehn, J.P.; Lupi, F.; Kaplowitz, M.D. 2003. Untying a Lancastrian bundle: valuing ecosystems and ecosystem services for wetland mitigation. Journal of Environmental Management. 68: 263–272.

Jack, B.K.; Kousky, C.; Sims, K. 2008. Designing payments for ecosystem services: lessons from previous experience with incentive-based mechanisms. Proceedings of the National Academy of Sciences. 105(28): 9465–9470.

Jenkins, M.; Scherr, S.; Inbar, M. 2004. Markets for biodiversity services: potential roles and challenges. Environment. 46(6): 34.

Kroeger, T.; Casey, F. 2007. An assessment of market-based approaches to providing ecosystem services on agricultural lands. Ecological Economics. 64: 321–332.

Land Trust Alliance, 2010. Easements: frequently asked questions. http:www.landtrustalliance.org/conservation/landowners/faqs-1/faq-conservation-easement/. (June 4, 2010).

Lien, A. 2010. Personal communication. Project director, Pinchot Institute. 1616 P Street NW, Suite 100. Washington, D.C. 20036

National Forest Foundation. 2010. Carbon Capital Fund. http://www.fs.fed.us/ecosystemservices/Carbon_Capital_Fund/faqs.shtml#whatis. (June 2, 2010).

Nelson, E.; Polasky, S.; Lewis, D.; Plantinga, A.; Lonsdorf, E.; White, D.; Bael, D.; Lawler, J. 2008. Efficiency of incentives to jointly increase carbon sequestration and species conservation on a landscape. Proceedings of the National Academy of Sciences. 105(28): 9471–9476.

Pagiola, S. 2007. Payments for environmental services in Costa Rica. http://mpra.ub.uni-muenchen.de/2010. (October 25, 2010).

Patterson, T.M.; Coelho, D.L. 2009. Ecosystem services: foundations, opportunities, and challenges for the forest products sector. Forest Ecology and Management. 257: 1637–1646.

Parsons, D. 2009. Carbon credits as match? http://blog.conservationregistry. org/2009/11/doug-parsons-carbon-credits-as-match/. (February 17, 2010).

Perrot-Maître, D.; Davis, P. 2001. Case studies of markets and innovative financial mechanisms for water services from forests. http://www.forest-trends. org/documents/files/doc_134.pdf. (October 22, 2010).

Pinchot Institute, 2010. The Bay Bank: testing market mechanisms for ecosystem restoration of Chesapeake forests. http://www.pinchot.org/current_projects/ baybank. (April 14, 2010).

Regional Greenhouse Gas Initiative, Inc. [RGGI]. 2007. Overview of the RGGI CO_2 budget trading program. http://www.rggi.org/docs/program_ summary_10_07.pdf. (January 12, 2010).

Ruddell, S.; Sampson, R.; Smith, M.; Giffen, R.; Cathcart, J.; Hagan, J.; Sosland, D.; Godbee, J.; Price, W.; Simpson, R. 2007. The role for sustainably managed forests in climate change mitigation. Journal of Forestry. 105(7): 314–319.

Ruhl, J.B.; Kraft, S.; Lant, C. 2007. The law and policy of ecosystem services. Washington, DC: Island Press: 96–109.

Salzman, J. 2005. Creating markets for ecosystem services: notes from the field. 80 N.Y.U. L. Rev. 870. New York: New York University Law Review. 897–900 p.

Salzman, J.; Thompson, B.; Daily, G. 2001. Protecting ecosystem services: science, economics and law. 20 Stan. Envtl. L.J. 309. California: Stanford University Environmental Law Journal. 319 p.

Sampson, R.N. 2004. Integrating land use, land use change, and forestry into a mandatory national greenhouse gas reduction program. In: Riggs, J.A., ed. A climate policy framework: balancing policy and politics. Queenstown, MD: The Aspen Institute: 63–72.

Sánchez-Azofeifa, G.A.; Pfaff, A.; Robalino, J.A.; Boomhower, J.P. 2007. Costa Rica's Payment for Environmental Services Program: intention, implementation, and impact. Conservation Biology. 21(5): 1166–1167.

Stavins, R.N. 1998. What can we learn from the grand policy experiment? Lessons from SO_2 allowance trading. Journal of Economic Perspectives. 12: 69–88.

Stavins, R.N. 2005. Lessons from SO$_2$ allowance trading. Choices. 20: 53–57.

Stein, S.M.; Alig, R.J.; White, E.M.; Comas, S.J.; Carr, M.; Eley, M.; Elverum, K.; O'Donnell, M.; Theobald, D.M.; Cordell, K.; Haber, J.; Beauvais, T.W. 2007. National forests on the edge: development pressures on America's national forests and grasslands. Gen. Tech. Rep. PNW-GTR-728. Portland, OR: U.S. Department of Agriculture, Forest Service, Pacific Northwest Research Station. 26 p.

Taylor, B. 2010. Personal communication. Oregon Biodiversity Program Director, Defenders of Wildlife, 1880 Willamette Falls Drive, Suite 200, West Linn, OR 97068.

United Nations Framework Convention on Climate Change [UNFCCC]. 2007. Kyoto Protocol: status of ratification. http://unfccc.int/kyoto_protocol/status_of_ratification/items/2613.php. (December 14, 2009).

United Nations Framework Convention on Climate Change [UNFCCC]. 2010. Clean Development Mechanism. http://cdm.unfccc.int/index.html. (December 14, 2009).

U.S. Department of Agriculture, Forest Service [USDA FS]. 2010. Budget. http://www.fs.fed.us/aboutus/budget/. (March 19, 2010).

U.S. Department of Agriculture, Forest Service [USDA FS]. 2007. Valuing ecosystem services: capturing the true value of nature's capital. http://www.fs.fed.us/ecosystemservices/pdf/ecosystem-services.pdf. (October 14, 2010).

U.S. Department of Agriculture, Natural Resources Conservation Service [NRCS]. 2010. Environmental Quality Incentives Program. http://www.nrcs.usda.gov/programs/eqip/index.html. (April 22, 2010).

U.S. Department of Agriculture, Natural Resources Conservation Service [NRCS]. 2009. Wetlands Reserve Program. http://www.nrcs.usda.gov/programs/WRP/. (November 16, 2009).

U.S. Environmental Protection Agency [U.S. EPA]. 2010a. Mitigation banking factsheet. http://www.epa.gov/wetlands/facts/fact16.html. (January 5, 2010).

U.S. Environmental Protection Agency [U.S. EPA]. 2010b. Wetlands compensatory mitigation. http://www.epa.gov/owow/wetlands/pdf/CMitigation.pdf. (January 5, 2010).

U.S. Green Building Council [USGBC]. 2010. Introduction: what LEED is. http://www.usgbc.org/DisplayPage.aspx?CMSPageID=1988. (March 19, 2010).

U.S. Fish and Wildlife Service. 2003. Guidance for the establishment, use and operation of conservation banks. http://www.fws.gov/endangered/esa-library/pdf/Conservation_Banking_Guidance.pdf. (October 21, 2010).

Willamette Partnership, 2009. About ecosystem services markets. http://willamettepartnership.org/about-markets/. (December 14, 2009).

Willamette Partnership, 2010. Ecosystem credit accounting. http://willamettepartnership.org/ecosystem-credit-accounting. (June 4, 2010).

www.ingramcontent.com/pod-product-compliance
Lightning Source LLC
Chambersburg PA
CBHW081135280526
45787CB00007B/3085